DRAWING FASHIONS

Don Bolognese & Elaine Raphael

DRAWING FASHIONS

Figures, Faces, and Techniques

Franklin Watts/New York/Toronto/London/Sydney/1985

To Betty and Lucy
who love to dress up
and go to the palace

Library of Congress Cataloging in Publication Data

Bolognese, Don.
Drawing fashions.

(A How-to-draw book)
Summary: Provides basic techniques for sketching
and drawing fashions, discusses materials, and analyzes
faces and figures.
1. Fashion drawing—Juvenile literature.   2. Fashion—
History—Juvenile literature.   [1. Fashion drawing]
I. Raphael, Elaine.   II. Title.
TT509.B65   1985   741.67′2   85-11543
ISBN 0-531-10049-9

CONTENTS

DRAWING FASHIONS

INTRODUCTION

Lights flash! The showroom throbs with the beat of rock music. Beautiful and elegant models walk the length of a raised platform. Each one pauses . . . and turns, her clothes swirling about. Her jewelry sparkles in the glow of the spotlights. The audience applauds. More flashing cameras go off, each burst highlighting the brilliance of sequins and rhinestones.

The show continues. Finally two models lead someone to the center of the stage . . . the designer, the person who is responsible for all this glitter and style! The applause reaches a crescendo. The designer has achieved the ultimate reward of the fashion world—a successful show!—a great new line of clothes! In short, a triumph!

This is the world of fashion. Today we associate it with all the technology of modern life: photography, television, and hi-tech audio and light effects. But fashion is an ancient fascination. Humans learned to dress and decorate themselves long before they learned to write. Fashion actually began when we discovered our ability to create art.

You might even say that our own bodies were our first canvases. We painted them, carved them, stuck holes in them, stretched them, and stained them in efforts to decorate ourselves. We hung animal claws around our necks. We perched elaborate feather arrangements on our heads. We even sewed ourselves into animal skins.

We did these things because we believed in magic. We believed that if we altered our appearance, we would somehow influence our surroundings: the animal we hunted would be easier to catch or the animal that was hunting us would be frightened away. Of course we wore clothes to protect ourselves from the elements, but we also believed that a person could show his or her importance by the number and value of ornaments and finery. Clothes protected us from the weather and from thorns and rocks and told the world something about ourselves and our society.

Truly, one can say that the history of fashion is really the story of mankind. It is a story that repeats itself with variations, over and over again. And now you are going to add your bit to that story. Who knows, maybe someday your illustrations and designs will add another glamorous chapter to fashion history.

CHAPTER ONE

Basic Materials

The fashion artist who achieves recognition works very hard to earn it. Although the fashion world is glamorous, it is also very demanding. A fashion artist can be expressive and stylish, but only if the fashion is presented convincingly. And a convincing fashion illustration requires strong figure drawing. Figure drawing begins with observation, a skill that is sharpened by sketching. And doing a great many quick sketches is the very best way to get started. While you are sketching don't use only one medium. Switch from pencil to felt pen or from pen to brush. You'll discover that each material will give you a different effect. This in turn will help you to develop a personal style (see chapters 5 and 6). But remember, the secret ingredient is lots of practice.

To begin you'll need to get together some basic materials. These are tools that will be useful for both your sketches and finished illustrations.

You will need: pencils, pens and pen points, felt-tip markers, brushes, various papers, ink, watercolors, erasers, a pencil sharpener, a drawing board or table, a ruler, a collection of fashion pictures, a mannequin or lifelike doll and—finally—some good friends who will be willing to pose for you.

Here are some specific suggestions:

Pencils

- No. 2 soft pencil—have a large number of sharpened ones when you are in a sketching session.

- A selection of drawing pencils from H (medium) up to 4B (soft and dark).

- A small box of conte crayons (black).

- A starter set of water-soluble colored pencils.

Pens and Pen Points

- A small pen holder for fine points such as the crow quill and a large holder for speedball type pen points.

Markers

- Black razor-point or fine-line tip—and larger chisel-edged markers in several shades of gray.

Brushes

- Good student-quality, pointed, sable type brushes: one each of #0, #3, and #7 (or as close to that as you can find).

Paper

- 14-by-17-inch pads of ordinary sketch bond, tracing, and newsprint papers; a few sheets of one-ply illustration paper with smooth surface (hot press) and medium surface (cold press); and a couple of sheets of medium weight watercolor paper.

Ink and Watercolors

- A jar each of black waterproof ink and black water-soluble ink.
- Transparent watercolors in either individual tubes or in small starter sets of assorted colors in cake or solid form.

Erasers

- Kneaded erasers. These work without much rubbing. Just press the eraser onto the pencil lines and it will lift off the lines. Knead the eraser so that a fresh surface is exposed. Repeat this. These erasers are also useful as a drawing tool. One use is lightening or creating highlights in pencil-shaded areas.

Drawing Table or Board

- Whether you have an adjustable drawing table or use a drawing board on a desk, make sure your drawing surface is tilted at an angle that is comfortable for you.

Picture Collection

- In addition to actual tools you will need reference material. These are pictures from magazines, newspapers, and books. These should be both photographic and illustrative. The pictures should include up-to-date fashions and past fashions. You should get at least one copy of *Women's Wear Daily*, a very influential fashion publication. Daily and Sunday newspapers are another excellent source of fashion illustrations. Also collect photos of your favorite fashion model(s) in as many different clothes and poses as possible.

Models for Figure Drawing

Good figure drawing can only be learned by drawing from a live model. Your friends can help you by posing for you. Try to get permission to draw during dance practice or ballet class. You should use a mirror to practice drawing views of the head and shoulders. And don't forget your local department stores. They often have fashion shows which should give you the opportunity to do quick sketches. And at the same time you'll be able to get the first look at latest fashions!

When live models are not available there are small artists' mannequins. These figures have moving parts so you can put them in fashion poses. You can drape material over them to see how an actual design looks. Also useful are lifelike dolls. The best practice, however, is sketching from a live model; try to do this at least once a week.

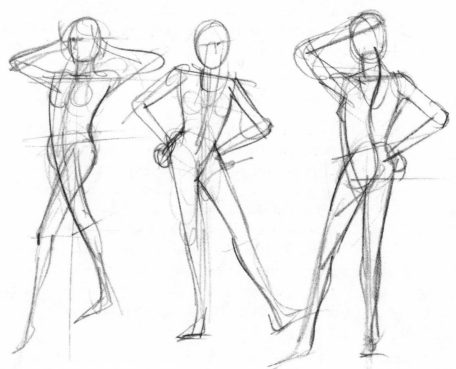

CHAPTER TWO

Sketching and Drawing

On the opposite page there is a series of quick sketches. None of them took more than a few seconds to do. Why work so fast? The answer: to train yourself to capture the most important lines in a pose. These are the lines that convey movement and posture. The movement or flow of a figure makes a drawing "come alive." The "posture" of a figure shows how different parts of the body relate to one another. Learning to identify these lines of movement and posture is essential to the fashion illustrator. Doing many quick sketches will develop your ability to "suggest" a pose with a minimum of lines.

This sketching is very different from drawings that convey a sense of both the texture and form of a particular fashion. These drawings, or "renderings," require another kind of observation, one that calls for a careful study of how fabrics appear when they are draped over and around the figure (see pages 20 and 21). This type of drawing takes more time because it requires a different kind of observation than you need for sketching. As you progress you will see that both the quick sketch and the drawing that takes more time are necessary to your artistic development.

Fashions today are less rigid than they were years ago. Fashion illustration must express this greater freedom of movement. These sketches will show you what to look for and what to emphasize in your sketches.

Note main action line.

The vertical line between neck base and foot position is a good way to check the balance of your figures. Figures that are out of balance appear to be tipping over.

[17]

These are very quick sketches of
models wearing loose-fitting clothes.
Disregard detail. Look for contrast
between body flow and clothing.
Note how the contours of the figure
are both revealed and hidden by
the clothes.

Take some simple fabrics—sheets or towels—and drape them over and around your model. These drawings give you some suggestions, but you should experiment with ideas of your own. The point of these drawings is to understand how fabrics affect the form of the model. Try using both light and heavy materials.

A good example of the relationship between fabric and the human form is the headdress—whether it is a hat, a shawl, a turban, or whatever. What we wear on our heads has often been the most different and eccentric aspect of our dress.

Girl with towel

A hat worn in medieval Europe

A 14th-century Italian headdress. Note how the ribbons emphasize the form.

This peaked hat with ribbon was a standard headdress for female factory workers during World War II.

Another turban type hat from France around 1920

A simple wide-brimmed hat. Note how the brim encircles the head.

You can learn much about form by doing a series of hat drawings. And you already have a good model who will sit for you as long as you wish—yourself. Get together a collection of hats and shawls, sit down in front of a mirror . . . and draw!

CHAPTER THREE

The Fashion Figure

Elegant. Elongate. These words sound similar. In the world of fashion illustration, they are almost identical. To create an *elegant* appearance, an artist must *elongate* the figure. This sounds easier than it is. Since live models have normal proportions, it is necessary to redesign figure drawings to achieve that elegance. On the next few pages you will see a normally proportioned figure grow into a long-limbed, graceful fashion figure.

This photo and the drawing at left are of the same model in the same pose. Note how the artist has changed the model's proportions to create a "fashion figure."

0

1

2

3

4

5

6

7

8

9

10

[26]

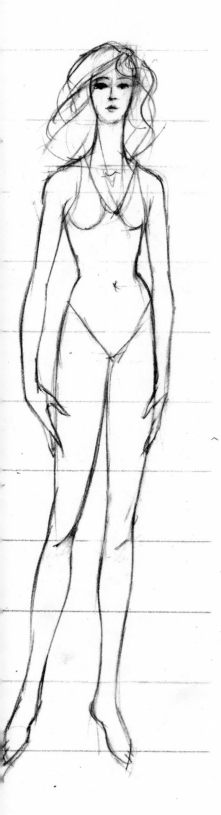

At first you will need guidelines to keep to the proper proportions. But with practice, this "new" figure will soon become "normal." The proportions of a fashion figure begin at eight heads and go to ten heads. These extremely elongated figures are used in high fashion styling.

This book uses the eight-head proportion. However, once you become used to drawing an elongated figure you will find it easy to vary its length to suit your specific fashion illustration. A figure is always lengthened in the legs and in the neck. The torso always stays the same. Put tracing paper over these figures and do *very quick* tracings. Practice this over and over and remember to keep your line loose. Don't fuss over details.

Typical Front Views

Note how the balance of the figure is maintained. Draw a line down from the base of the neck. That line should fall between the model's feet. When the weight is on one foot the line should go from the base of the neck to the heel.

Two other important lines are the hip and shoulder lines. Note that the higher hip and lower shoulder are usually on the same side of the figure.

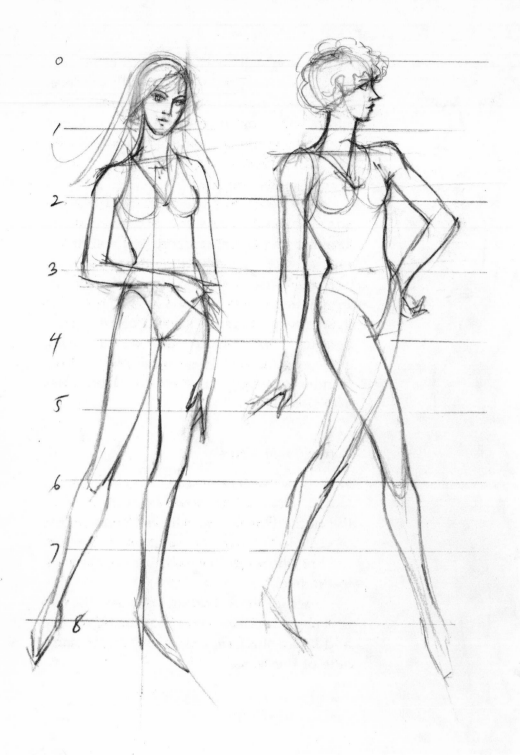

0

1

2

3

4

5

6

7

8

Side views often convey action.

Sometimes the shoulders are turned to the front. This creates a slimmer silhouette around the waist and hips.

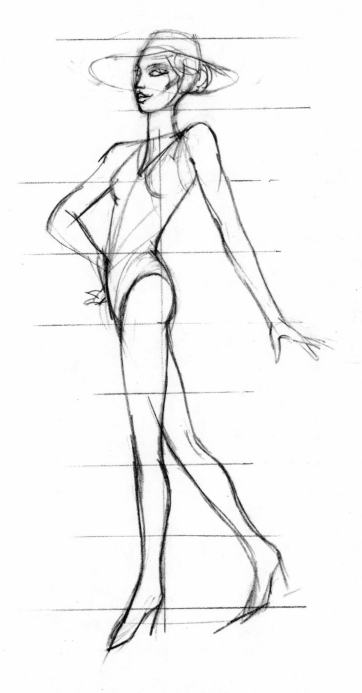

And remember the balance rule: Keep the base of the neck over the space between the feet. If your drawings seem to be tipping over, you are probably not observing that guideline.

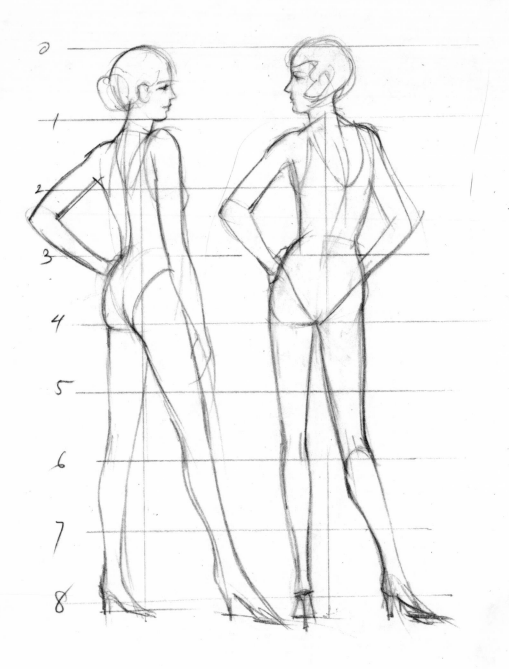

0

1

2

3

4

5

6

7

8

Back views are especially useful for showing evening gowns and bathing suits. Again, note the hip and shoulder lines.

A view that combines a side view of the shoulders with a side view of the legs and hips does two things: it avoids the problem of foreshortening the legs and it shows off the garment to its best advantage.

Drawing Men

A man's proportions in fashion drawings are similar to a woman's (eight to eight and a half heads). However, the upper body, shoulders, and chest are wider and the torso is longer. The neck is shorter and thicker. The limbs should have some muscle definition—but don't make the figures look like weight lifters.

Drawing Young People

Drawings of young people should include active poses and in general look less "posed." Life sketching is the best way to prepare for this. Do many five- and ten-second poses. Remember: Focus on the main action lines (see chapter 2).

You will want to practice the typical fashion poses in this chapter until you can do them very easily.

One way to add variety to your drawings without changing the basic pose is by changing the position of the head. You can do that by tracing the head from one figure and placing it on another. By using your file of fashion pictures as a guide you can experiment with different combinations until you find ones that look natural.

[38]

CHAPTER FOUR

Fashion Faces

Fashion faces are even more of a challenge than the figure. Although they must be elegant and stylish as well, each face must have enough distinction so that all the drawings don't look as if they were drawn from the same model. This is where a good file of fashion model photographs will be helpful.

The fashion face fits into a narrow rectangle. The outline is an egg-shaped oval with a slightly smaller end. That smaller end is the chin. Features are placed symmetrically, with the eyes at the halfway point. The tip of the nose is two-thirds down from the top. And when placing the mouth, leave enough room for a full, well-rounded chin.

Practice these steps over and over. When you feel comfortable drawing this face you can begin experimenting with slight variations.

Check through your file of fashion photos and select models that have unusual features. This will help your drawings have character.

A point to remember: Keep a light touch when drawing the front view of the nose. And in general it is wise to avoid heavy outlining and too many lines in drawing the female fashion face.

One more bit of advice: Keep up to date on cosmetics and hairstyling. Your fashion face must be as stylish as the clothes on the figure.

Note that the drawings of eyes and mouth also depend on symmetry.

[41]

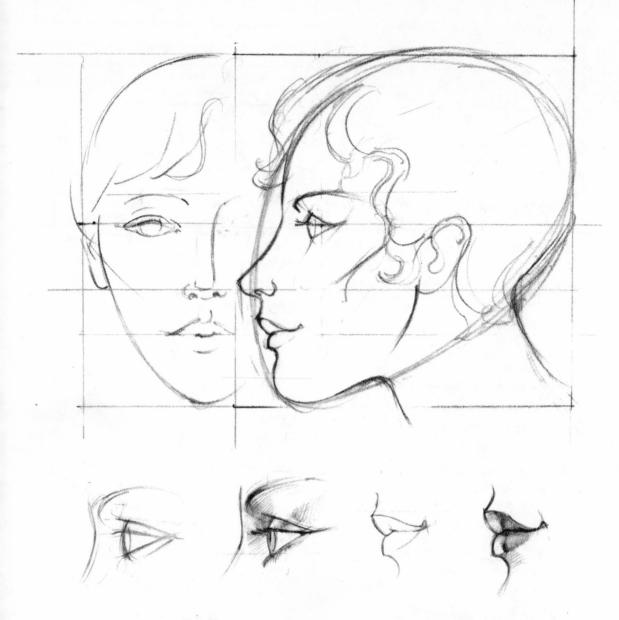

Profiles

A square is the basic guide. Divide it the same way you did the front view. After you have achieved some success with the contour lines add light tones around the eyes, at the temple, and under the cheekbone.

There are two other profiles you should practice. Follow the same procedure as on page 40 for experimenting with variations.

Note that the nostrils show when the head is tilted up.

[43]

Learning to draw the three-quarter view of the head is necessary if you want your fashion illustrations to look completely natural. But it is more difficult. However, with practice—especially drawing from life—you can produce convincing drawings.

Begin with a square. Use the same basic guidelines as you used for feature placement. The important thing to remember is that half the face is going away from you. This requires foreshortening of the eyes and the lips on that side.

Drawing a light profile line down the center of the forehead, over the nose, mouth, and chin will help you relate this view to the pure profile. And remember to use slightly curved guidelines when placing features on the three-quarter face.

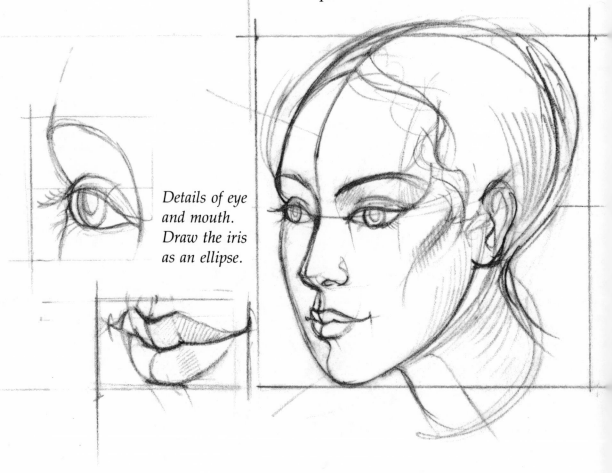

Details of eye and mouth. Draw the iris as an ellipse.

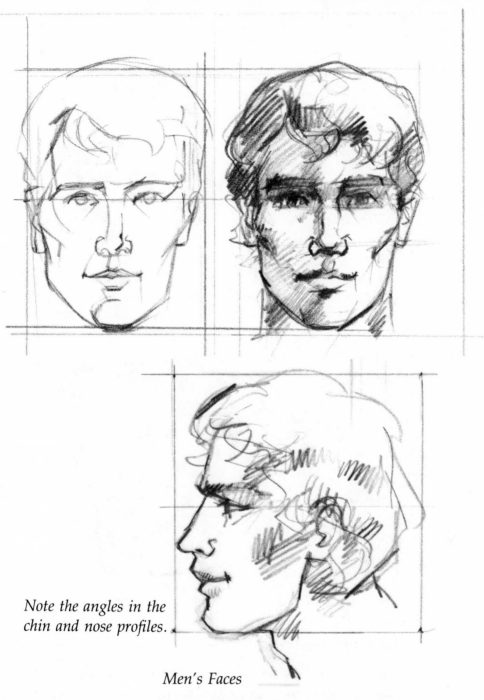

Note the angles in the chin and nose profiles.

Men's Faces

The basic proportions are the same as a woman's face. However, the basic contour is rectangular, with more angles and less curves. The lines are bolder; the shading is heavier.

[45]

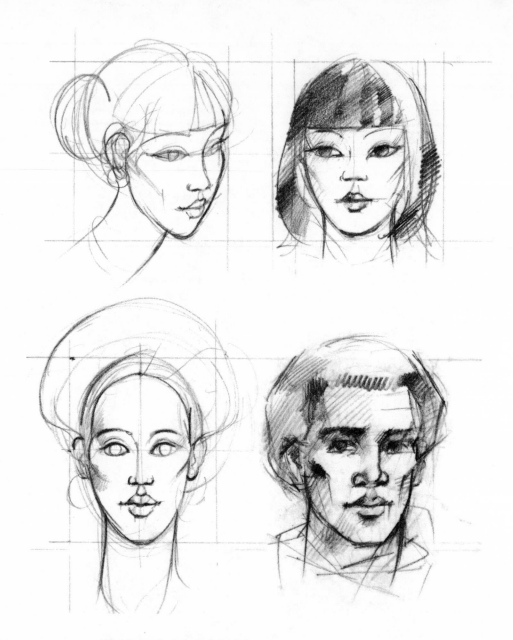

Black and Asian Models

All cultures and races are part of the fashion scene. Inspiration comes from Japan and Africa as well as from Paris and New York. The Asian model's face is slightly broader and flatter across the eyes. The cheekbones are higher and the lips full but short in length. The black model's face is a long oval with high cheekbones and full lips.

H

2B

6B

CHAPTER FIVE

Techniques and Textures

A "technique" is a method of using a tool. Artists try to develop a personal approach to a technique. This is called a style. Style makes their work recognizable. However, all artists, famous or not, use the same range of materials. Take, for example, the pencil.

Pencil

The pencil is probably the most useful and easy-to-use drawing tool in existence. It's safe to say that 70 percent or 80 percent of all your drawing will be done with one kind of pencil or another.

In fashion illustration a pencil is an especially useful tool because it can create the most detailed areas of pattern and textures as well as the roughest of sketches. And pencils come in a great variety: hard, soft, deep blacks, and silvery grays. There are charcoal pencils for use on textured paper, and there are even colored pencils that turn into watercolors.

To begin your experiments sharpen several kinds of pencils—and have a selection of papers ready (see chapter 1).

6B
side of pencil

PENCIL

Now do a series of strokes using both the point and the side of the pencil. Notice the variations in the shaded textures that can be achieved by simply using different papers.

4B
6B

paper with slight texture

6B

Watercolor paper

4B 6B
on smooth
surface
HB

*A very quick, stylized drawing
to indicate different fabrics.
Note how the side of the pencil
is used to indicate pleats.*

lace   plaid   pleats

pen & ink

Pen and Ink

What's the biggest difference between pen and ink and pencil? You're right! You can't erase a pen-and-ink line. And that makes working with pen and ink just a bit scarier. So why use them? Well, because pen and ink provide certain effects and textures that pencils do not. And there's one other reason important to your development as a fashion artist: working in a direct, non-erasable medium will help you become more confident of your ability. Of course you'll make mistakes—all artists do. But when you finally do a crisp, sharp pen-and-ink drawing that is just right, you will feel terrific.

Therefore, a good deal of experimenting is necessary. Begin by selecting three different pen points (see chapter 1), and a variety of papers from very smooth (ledger bond) to slightly rough and absorbent. Use two kinds of ink, waterproof and water soluble. Now do a series of cross-hatchings using all the pen points and both inks.

Take a clean brush and brush clear water over some of the crosshatched areas. Notice the effect on the water-soluble ink. Does this suggest ideas for drawing textures?

Pen and ink is also a very good tool for rendering detail. Pick two or three patterns. Draw them with a fine pen point on a smooth paper.

Brush

If pencil and pen are different they are still alike in one way. Each has a rigid point. Pencils and pens seem like natural extensions of our fingers. This gives us a feeling of control. However, because of its flexibility and bulk, a brush is more unpredictable.

Even the smallest sable watercolor brush can produce a thin hairline one instant and a thicker stroke the next. But it is this variation that gives a brush line its special quality—and the artist a special challenge.

Learning to control the brush will take practice. But treat the experience as fun. After working with a pencil, switch to a brush. Your line will begin to flow.

Felt-Tip Pen

A felt-tip pen is a great sketching medium. First use the wide tipped marker (see chapter 1) for broad gray strokes. Then draw over those with a pointed black marker. Working with these markers will help you to develop a sketchy style. Remember you can't erase so don't worry if a drawing doesn't turn out well. Just do another—and another.

FELT pen

CHAPTER SIX

Fashions in History

The time is fifty thousand years ago. A lone hunter is returning to his den, a cave somewhere in the south of France. It is autumn. There is a chill in the air. The hunter pulls the leather thong that hangs from the garment around his shoulders. The thong draws the fur piece closer to his body. He feels warmer . . .

A young woman strolls along the bank of the river Seine. It is November and overcast. She reaches up and draws one end of her cloak over her shoulder, making the garment fit more snugly. "That feels much better," she says as she walks briskly down the cobblestone path . . .

The cloak is a garment with a long history—and you can add a bit to that history by designing your own version. The steps you take to do this can be followed in designing any article of clothing.

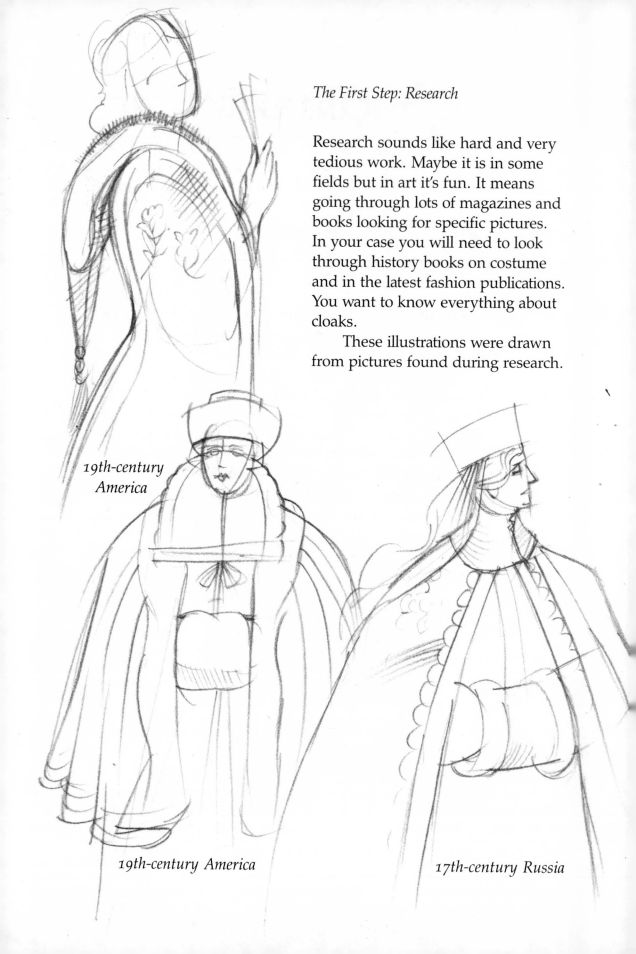

The First Step: Research

Research sounds like hard and very
tedious work. Maybe it is in some
fields but in art it's fun. It means
going through lots of magazines and
books looking for specific pictures.
In your case you will need to look
through history books on costume
and in the latest fashion publications.
You want to know everything about
cloaks.

These illustrations were drawn
from pictures found during research.

*19th-century
America*

19th-century America

17th-century Russia

14th-century Germany   19th-century America   14th-century Italy

The Second Step: Exploratory Sketches

Each period of fashion seems to have its own distinctive silhouette. In the mid-1980s the silhouette is a wide shoulder with a downward taper. You should consider this silhouette as a possibility.

The Third Step: The Final Design

Your design shows both the influence of
history and current fashions. And as you do
more drawings and more designs you will
find that ideas are coming to you faster than
you can put them down. The whole world
of fashion will be there waiting for you.

ABOUT THE AUTHOR

Don Bolognese and Elaine Raphael have written and illustrated almost 200 books for young readers and adults. Their collaborative efforts also include painting, graphic design, calligraphy, and, most recently, computer graphics.

They have won awards from the American Institute of Graphic Arts, the Bologna Bookfair, the Society of Illustrators, and many others.

They live and work in both Vermont and New York City.